Table of Contents

Crypto Teacher welcomes you to a new Digital Financial System 2021

Investing in Crypto

Trump signs Executive 13772 Bringing in the New Economy

U.S. DEPARTMENT OF THE TREASURY
A Financial System

That Creates Economic
Opportunities
Nonbank Financials, Fintech, and
Innovation

Report to President Donald J.
Trump
Executive Order 13772 on Core
Principles
for Regulating the United States
Financial System

Secretary Steven T. Mnuchin
Counselor to the Secretary Craig S.
Phillips

What is Bitcoin (BTC)

Bitcoin -is a cryptocurrency. It is a decentralized digital currency without a central bank or single administrator that can be sent from user to user on the peer-to-peer bitcoin network without the need for intermediaries. Transactions are verified by network nodes through cryptography and recorded in a public distributed ledger called a blockchain.

How does Bitcoin work- Bitcoins are traded from one personal wallet to another. A wallet is a small personal database that you store on your computer, smartphone or tablet. Bitcoin is a cryptocurrency that is not physical Bitcoin is basically software. You can own one Bitcoin or fractions of a Bitcoin. Users can keep Bitcoin in their digital wallets, as well as sell, buy, and send them to other people. Every transaction is recorded on a public ledger called the blockchain which can't be tampered with or changed. Transactions are finalized quickly and securely from one peer to another. Everything happens without a third party like banks or other financial institutions.

Purpose of Bitcoin-Bitcoin acts as digital gold. Protecting you from deflationary fiat currencies as we see today across the globe. Bitcoin is simply an accounting ledger just in code (computer language). This code makes it impossible for users to modify records without being caught, as any change would alter the network and the block would be rejected. Bitcoin is generated every time a new block is validated and added to the blockchain. It's a process called mining that requires a large amount of computational power. Miners use specific hardware to solve the complex mathematical puzzles necessary to validate blocks and receive Bitcoin in return. The Bitcoin blockchain was built to generate a total of 21 million Bitcoin. This means that only 21 million can ever exist. It cannot be printed like fiat currency and its scarcity increases its value while protecting users against inflation.

Alt-coins

Alt-coins are the alternative cryptocurrency's over than <u>Bitcoin</u>. Many alt-coins are trying to target any perceived limitations that Bitcoin has and come up with newer versions with competitive advantages. As the term 'alt-coins' means all cryptocurrencies which are not Bitcoin, there are hundreds of alt-coins.

Alt-coins

Biggest alt-coins you may have heard of include Ethereum, Ripple, Bitcoin Cash, Litecoin, and Monero.

Ether: Ether is the cryptocurrency generated by the Ethereum platform, so this cryptocurrency is often also called Ethereum. The Ethereum platform is a ledger technology other companies can build on. For example, JP Morgan Chase, Microsoft, Intel, Mastercard, Credit Suisse and BP have tested Ethereum platform.

Ripple (XRP): Ripple who coin is called XRP, is owned by a private company. Technically, the company is named Ripple and the tokens are named XRP. Over 500 banks are using Ripple to settle cross-border payments , but they're basically just sending digital IOUs and settling with traditional money later rather than actually using the XRP tokens. Ripple will be the new SWIFT

Bitcoin Cash: This was originally a fork of Bitcoin, but is now a separate currency, despite the name. The changes that were made are faster transactions and low fees compared to Bitcoin

Litecoin: Litecoin was also originally a fork of Bitcoin as well. Litecoin uses a different proof-of-work algorithm. The network tries to complete a block four times as often as Bitcoin, which is designed to speed up transaction confirmation.

Monero: Monero is designed to be a privacy coin. Transactions on the blockchain can't be traced back to individual users like cash.

Definitions of Crypto

Trading Related Terms

Exchanges -Websites where you can buy and sell crypto-currencies. Some popular exchanges in North America are: Coinbase

FIAT-Government-issued currency, such as the US dollar.

Whale - Someone that owns absurd amounts of crypto-currency.

Limit order - buy or sell- Orders placed by traders to buy or sell a crypto-currency when the price meets a certain amount. They can be thought of as 'for-sale' signs. These orders are what are bought and sold against when traders place market orders.

Sell wall / buy wall- Using a chart, traders can see the current limit buy and sell points. The graphics on the depth chart looks like walls

Market order -buy or sell- A simple purchase or sale of a token on an exchange at the current price. Market buys purchase the cheapest crypto you purchased available on the order book, and market sells fill the most expensive buy order on the books.

Margin trading- Trades by risking your existing coins. (NOTE: Very risky, only for experienced traders and only on certain exchanges even then)

Going long- A margin trade that profits if the price increases.
Going short- A margin trade that profits if the price decreases.

Bullish- Price is going to increase.

Bearish- Price is going to decrease.

ATH- meaning All Time High

Altcoin- Any crypto-currency other than Bitcoin

Tokens- are created on existing blockchains, anyone can make their own custom token on Bitcoin or Ethereum blockchain

ICO- Initial Coin Offering, somewhat similar to an IPO in the non-crypto world. Startups issue their own token in exchange for ether. This is essentially crowdfunding on the ethereum platform.

Pump and Dump- Normally a whale (someone who holds or buys a lot of a certain currency). Then dumps it to make a lot of money

Stable coin- a crypto normally pegged to fiat currency to decrease volatility.

Crypto arbitrage - Taking advantage of a difference in price of the same crypto on two different exchanges. Buy low on one exchange and sell high on another.

FOMO- Fear Of Missing Out. The need to get on the train when the price of something starts to skyrocket.

FUD- Fear, Uncertainty, and Doubt. Negativity spread intentionally by someone that wants the price of something to drop.

Bagholder- Someone holding an altcoin after a pump and dump crash. A coin that is sinking in value with few future prospects.

Market Cap- The total value held in a crypto-currency. It is calculated by multiplying the total supply of coins by the current price of an individual unit.

ROI- Return on Investment. The percentage of how much money has been made compared to an initial investment.

TA- Trend Analysis or Technical Analysis. Refers to the process of examining current charts in order to predict which way the market will move next.

MACD- Moving Average Convergence Divergence. A trend indicator that shows the relationship between two moving averages of prices.

Bollinger Band- A margin around the price of a crypto that helps indicate when a coin is overbought or oversold.

Basic Cryptocurrency Terms

blockchain- Blockchains are distributed ledgers, secured by cryptography. They are essentially public databases that everyone can access and read, but the data can only be updated by the data owners. Instead of the data residing on a single centralized server, the data is copied across thousands and thousands of computers worldwide.

Node- A computer that possesses a copy of the blockchain and is working to maintain it.

Mining- The process of trying to 'solve' the next block. It requires obscene amounts of computer processing power to do effectively, but is rewarded.

Mining rig- A computer especially designed for processing proof-of-work blockchains, like Bitcoin. They often consist of multiple high-end graphic processors (GPUs) to maximize their processing power.

Fork A situation where a blockchain splits into two separate chains. Forks generally happen in the crypto-world when new 'governance rules' are built into the blockchain's code.

PoW meaning proof of work. The current algorithm used by Ethereum.

PoS-Proof-of-stake -The proposed future consensus algorithm to be used by crypto. Instead of mining in its current form, people that own a certain crypto will be able to 'lock up' their crypto for a short amount of time in order to 'vote' and generate network consensus. The plan is that these stakeholders will be rewarded with crypto by doing so.

Sharding- A scaling solution for blockchains. Typically, every node in a blockchain network houses a complete copy of the blockchain. Sharding is a method that allows nodes to have partial copies of the complete blockchain in order to increase overall network performance and consensus speeds.

Software wallet- Storage for crypto-currency that exists purely as software files on a computer. Software wallets can be generated for free from a variety of sources.

Hardware wallet- A device that can securely store crypto-currency. Hardware wallets are often regarded as the most secure way to hold crypto-currency.

Cold storage- The process of moving crypto-currency 'offline', as a way of safekeeping your crypto-currency from hacking.

Ethereum Specific Terms

Smart contract- Code that is deployed onto the Ethereum blockchain. They allow a transaction without a third party by verifying and enforcing performance on the contract.

Solidity- One of the most popular languages that smart contracts can be written in.

Dapp- Decentralized Application. Has its back-end code running on a decentralize peer to peer network.

The Flippening- Where a low market cap becomes higher than a market cap above them. Example XRP and Ethereum changed places a few times.

Gas- is the execution fee for every operation made on ethereum blockchain.

Gas price- The amount of ether to be spent for each gas unit on a transaction.

Memes

Hodl- Hold on to your crypto know matter what happens

Mooning- Price makes a massive move up

Longest bull run on stock market and economic expansion in history is now coming to an end along with the dollar

The United States debt is 27 trillion and growing. The global debt is 274 trillion dollars. The economic growth cycle is coming to an end. There is a reason why they don't teach economics in the U.S. If you knew how the economy worked the system wouldn't work.

The stock market is owned by a small group of people 70% of the stock market is owned by the wealthy top 10%. The tax cuts that Trump approved led to Trillions of buybacks which are keeping the stock market bubble going. With interest rates going up it will cause the yield to invert. Every time this happens its a signal for a collapse of the economy.

The elderly and baby-boomers are not making any money on their saving due to the lowest interest rates in history. While they have to work longer and the rich keeps getting richer.

All the major Corporations are invested in crypto
So why aren't you?

Facebook says it hopes to reach 100 founding members before the official Libra launch and it's open to anyone that meets the requirements, including direct competitors like Google or Twitter.

Vechain Corporate Partnerships

is a blockchain-enabled platform that is designed to enhance supply chain management processes.

China National Level partnership,Direct Imported Goods (D.I.G)
China Unicom, Kuehne & Nagel, DB Schenker, BMW Group, LVMH
Groupe Renault, Fanghuwang, iTaotaoke, Bright Food, LogSafer
Shanghai eGrid Consulting Co. LTD, NTT Docomo

People's Insurance Company
of China (PICC), BYD
SBTG Surplus & Co, ENN
Energy Holdings Limited
Republic of Cyprus National
Level partnership, Fuji
MARUMO Tea
Baijie Teng IoT Technology
Corporation, BIOS Middle East
Reebonz Holding Limited,
Haier, Norway in a Box,
Walmart China

Ripple Corporate Partnerships

Banks

American Express, Standard
Chartered, Bank of America Merrill
Lynch, PNC Financial Services,
Cuallix, Catalyst Corporate Federal
Credit Union, Star One Credit
Union, CBW Bank, Cross River
Bank

Royal Bank of Canada, DH
Corporation, Canadian Imperial
Bank of Commerce, Scotiabank,
Bank of Montreal, ATB Financial

TD Bank Canada, Saldo, Interbank,
Euro Exim Bank

Bank of England (Central bank),
HSBC, Barclays, Vitesse

Royal Bank of Scotland, Credit
Agricole, Natixis, Banco Santander

BBVA, Banca Intesa Sanpaolo,
UniCredit, Reise Bank, Fidor Bank
Rabobank, Erste Group AG, UBS,
Credit Suisse, Nordea
Skandinaviska Enskilda Banken
AB, Akbank, Bank Leumi Le-Israel
National Bank of Kuwait
Kuwait Finance House
Bank Dhofar, Saudi Arabian
Monetary Authority (Central bank)
First Bank of Abu Dhabi, RakBank,
Al Rajhi Bank, DBS Group
OCBC Bank, United Overseas
Bank, Singapore Exchange,
Krungsri
Bank of Thailand (Central bank),
Bank of Indonesia (Central bank)
Siam Commercial Bank, Cargills
Bank, Kotak Mahindra Bank

IndusInd Bank, Axis Bank, Yes
Bank, Faysal Bank, Shanghai
Huarui Bank, Woori Bank, SBI
Holdings, Mitsubishi UFJ Financial
Group
Fukui Bank, Star Bank, Aomori
Bank, Ashikaga Bank, Awa Bank
AEON Bank, Senshu Ikeda Bank,
Iyo Bank, Oita Bank, Orix Bank
Gumma Bank, Keiyo Bank, San-In
Godo Bank, Sikoku Bank, 77 Bank
Shimizu Bank, Juroku Bank,
Shinkin Central Bank, Shinsei Bank
Hachijuni Bank, Michinoku Bank,
Mizuho Financial Group,
Musashino Bank, Nomura Trust
and Banking Company, Seven
Bank, Sony Bank

Yachiyo Bank, Tochigi Bank, Bank of the Ryukyus, Chiba Bank Chugoku bank, Daishi Bank, Daiwa Next Bank,Hiroshima Bank Hyakugo Bank, Suruga Bank, Yamaguchi Bank, Hokuriku Bank Nishi-Nippon City Bank, North Pacific Bank, Resona Bank Shikoku Bank, Sumitomo Mitsui Trust Bank, Toho Bank, Tsukuba Bank, Yamagata Bank,Bank of Yokohama,SBI Sumishin Net Bank ANZ, Westpac, Commonwealth Bank of Australia, Macquarie Group National Australia Bank

Remittance/Money Transfer Firms

American Express FX International Payments, InstaRem, SendFriend Beetech, Viamericas, Transpaygo, UniPAY, MoneyGram, Zip Remit Itau Unibanco, Western Union, UAE Exchange, TransferGo, SBI Remit, FlashFX, Earthport

Foreign Exchange Companies

Currencies Direct, FairFX, RationalFX, Exchange4Free, Bexs Banco,
eZforex, FlashFX

Cryptocurrency Exchanges

Coin-one
SBI Virtual Currencies

Payments Providers

Mercury FX
Cambridge Global Payments
Finastra, Davis + Henderson (D+H),
Finable, LianLian Pay
IDT
GoLance
AirWallex
Dlocal
TAS Group
Software/Technology
MoneyMatch
Volante
Expertus
Temenos
CGI Group
Yantra Financial Technologies
Miscellaneous
Deloitte
Accenture

Arrington XRP Capital
We Make Price
Selly
The Asia MTM Group
IDT
Bichip

History Lesson

The American people were not taught finances for a reason in public school. The U.S. dollar came off the gold standard by President Nixon. President Nixon and Henry Kissinger signed a deal with the Saudi's to create the Petro Dollar. The Saudi's would only settle their oil in U.S. dollars. That's how the U.S. Emperor began. It allowed the creation of the middle class. Now over 40 years later the Saudi's are moving away from oil and countries are moving away from the U.S. Dollar.

Gold

Let's you know the real value of your paper money

The price of gold remained remarkably stable for long periods of time. For example, Sir Isaac Newton, as master of the U.K. Mint, set the gold price at L3.17s. 10d. per troy ounce in 1717, and it remained effectively the same for two hundred years until 1914. The only exception was during the Napoleonic wars from 1797 to 1821. The official U.S. Government gold price has changed only four times from 1792 to the present. Starting at $19.75 per troy ounce, raised to $20.67 in 1834, and $35 in 1934. In 1972, the price was raised to $38 and then to $42.22 in 1973. A two-tiered pricing system was created in 1968, and the market price for gold has been free to fluctuate.

Contact us:

WWW.BTCTEACHER.COM

Where can you buy?
https://www.coinbase.com/join/
59472d40816b990a82024aee
 https://www.binance.us/?
ref=35042444 The two companies
we recommend but there are
several Exchanges to choose from.
Coinbase is user friendly.

R.E.B.E.L.
Ripple, Ethereum, Bitcoin, EOS and Litecoin

Made in the USA
Middletown, DE
04 January 2021